# *but* JESUS

## a conversation

### AUTUMN MCALPIN

pink umbrella
books

## *Praise for But Jesus: A Conversation*

"Encircle has worked with thousands of LGBTQ+ youth. Tragically, most of them struggle with mental health issues and suicidality. Let's be clear—these issues do not exist because these children are LGBTQ; it is because of the negative, harmful and dangerous messages they grow up hearing about themselves. This dangerous and destructive narrative must stop. Kids are literally dying. When these precious children are within the circles of our families' and communities' love, they will thrive, and we will all be better for it. Within these pages, we see a family fully encircle their LGBTQ+ child in unconditional love. Each line unfolds the pain, joy, growth, and complexity of a family's courageous journey. This book will serve as a compass for thousands of families."

- Stephenie Larsen, founder and CEO of Encircle

"Decided to read one or two pages before rushing out the door. 20 pages. 30 pages. 60 pages. Brilliant, disturbing, comforting. A significant gift to those who are—or will be—facing the LDS/LGBTQ dilemma. A powerful indictment of—and invitation to—those who choose judgment over love."

- Carol Lynn Pearson, author of *No More Goodbyes*; *Goodbye, I Love You*; *Finding Mother God*; *I'll Walk With You*; *The Love Map*

"Autumn McAlpin's poetry shows us the heart of things. The heart of a thorny doctrinal debate, the heart of our most anguished spiritual yearnings, the heart that is wounded by betrayal, the mother's heart that will fight for her beloved child. If you have a queer child or know someone who has a queer child (and you do), read this book and pass it on."

- Amy McPhie Allebest, podcaster, *Breaking Down Patriarchy*

"Filmmaker and storyteller Autumn McAlpin's vulnerable memories pull the reader into the aching heart of a mother trying to raise a healthy gay child while reevaluating all she's been taught as a member of the Church of Jesus Christ of Latter-day Saints. *But Jesus: A Conversation* invites the reader to better understand the precarious balance between Church and child, walked by so many families today."

- Allison Dayton, founder of Lift + Love

"I'm grateful for the courage of my friend Autumn McAlpin for sharing their family story of loving and supportive their gay son Gavin. This is a beautiful family love story. It's also a story of how we can do better to love, support, and value our queer family and friends. I wish I had read a book like this earlier in my life as an active Latter-day Saint. When we know better, we do better. I encourage you to read this book and then consider what you can do in your circle of influence to better support queer Latter-day Saints and their families as we work to create Zion. A Zion where we all are needed and should feel a deep sense of belonging."

- Richard Ostler, podcaster and author of *Listen, Learn and Love*

All proceeds from the sales of this book will be donated to therapy funds at Encircle and Flourish, both 501c3 organizations that provide mental health services for LGBTQ+ youth and young adults.

Scan to donate
to Encircle

Scan to donate
to Flourish

For Gavin

*"Not everything that is faced can be changed,*
*but nothing can be changed until it is faced."*
*- James Baldwin*

# Table of Contents

## Confession

*I have something to tell you,*
Says my 17-year-old son at 3 a.m.
*A few things actually:*
*1) I'm gay.*
*2) I'm done with the church.*
*3) I've really been struggling with depression. Like... really.*

## Cause and Effect

This is the order in which they pierce:
*1) I've really been struggling with depression. Like... really.*
*2) I'm done with the church.*
*3) I'm gay.*

In this order, the new order of my universe, I break it down:
What caused one? Was it two or three?
What caused two? Was it one or three?
The three itself, I welcome; in this, he exhales peace.
Part of me always anticipated the three.

## A Child's Prayer

*Heavenly Father, are you really there?*
*And do you [really] answer every child's prayer?*

I silently scream, after he leaves the room.

# Things They Said

"Did you always know?"

"See your little guy out there, jumping on the trampoline in a princess dress?
All I can say is, don't ask, don't tell."

"Arguably the brightest student I've ever had. But at recess, he struggles to connect..."

"Taekwondo!? Sign him up for a real sport!"

"He really just prefers Legos."

"Tell him to ask Mia or Zoe!? They're looking for dates!"

"Have you always known?"

"Not everyone's into team sports."

"Sometimes they're just late bloomers."

"My kid hated dances, too."

"Jenna or Abby?"

"Promise me when I go off to college, you'll figure him out."

"There's got to be someone he'd want to go out with!"

"You know why he's depressed, right?
He's gay. I did my dissertation on homosexuality. I know these things."

"What kind of high school junior wants to spend his spring break
with his mom painting tulips in the Netherlands?"

"Promise me when I'm on my mission, you'll figure him out."

"I've known it since he was three. I never said anything because
sometimes... I'm wrong."

"All I can say is God makes them the way they come,
and God don't make no mistakes."

"I'd strongly encourage him to wait until he graduates to fully come out.
High schoolers can be brutal."

"You knew, right?"

### *Things I Said*

A perfect baby.
Perfect child.
Never screamed.
Never cried.
Never did a thing wrong in his life.
Mama's boy.
Teacher's pet.
Schoolwide standout.
Future prophet?

## *Things He Did*

How he tried.
How he tried.
How he tried so hard to hide.

He sat up front
All smiles and nods
And beat himself
With unseen rods.
Not for what
He's said or done
But what he feared
He might become.
If he stopped
The pleading smiles
The nodding, blending, self-denial
The retching, sobbing floods, the writhing
All from a youth of
Constant hiding.

# *Fear*

Heights

Spiders

Public Speaking

Elevators

Airplanes

Snakes

Lice

The first day of school

The stomach flu

Wrinkles

Driving on the freeway

Swimming in lakes

Swallowing gum

Going bald

The dark

Your family and friends finding out who you are.

Dying inside because they do not yet know.

# Off a Bridge

The hotline says it's probably not real unless they have a plan.
You're supposed to ask them about their plan.
That night, he didn't mention a plan.
And I didn't ask.
I couldn't.
It was a lot to process at once, the #1, the #2, the #3.
But regarding the plan, I have had to ask others:
three friends, two relatives.
One I asked about the details only after her plan didn't work.
We now celebrate her "Lucky Day."
I contemplated his plan, if there even was one.
We had bottles, but not enough pills
A gun, but no bullets
A rope, did we still have that rope?
He was 17, driving for a year; he knew where stores were.
He could find a plan.
But I only kind of asked.
Because you only kind of want to know.
If you don't fully know, then it's not fully real.
A few months later, when I thought things were better, but triggers
still happened (no, not that kind), he told me his plan, and I
understood there had always been a plan.
Maybe more of a daydream, a mirage, a what if
Like the postpartum mother who dangles her baby over the balcony.

He would drive off a bridge in our town.

I'm not sure that would even work,
I often think at 3 a.m.

## Back to the Two

*2) I'm done with the church,*
He says.
*I believe in the gospel of Jesus Christ,*
He says.
*I believe in Jesus,*
He says.
*But there is no healthy place for me in the church.*
He says.

## He Read That

*"I said that they [homosexuals] should be excommunicated without any doubt, that the homosexual has no right to membership in the Church..."*
\- President David O. McKay, 1965

*"Let this individual repent of his perversion, force himself to return to normal pursuits and interest and actions and friendships with the opposite sex, and this normal pattern can become natural again."*
\- President Spencer W. Kimball, 1969

*"The person who teaches or condones the crimes for which Sodom and Gomorrah were destroyed — we have coined a softer name for them than came from old; we now speak of homosexuality."*
– J. Reuben Clark, Jr., 1952

He read all that. Years before you did. Don't tell him how to feel.

## But That's Not True!

They say. They say.
*We've come a long way! We've changed since Prop 8!*
*Look at our website: Mormonandgay.org!*
*There is room on our benches;*
*We are all told to love.*
*We do not judge.*
*We do not judge.*
*There is no sin in being,*
*Only in doing.*\*
*He can still come*
*Just maybe not talk about it.*\*
*He can still serve the ward.*
*But not among children.*\*
*We need him! We need him!*
*As long as he doesn't live the lifestyle or promote the agenda.*\*
*We all have to obey the law of chastity.*
(But for him, law of celibacy?)
*Think of all the unmarried 50-year-olds.*
(Who live with hope.)
*It's like my grandchild with autism. She can't be married.*
(But if she could…)
*We all have challenges.*
(For a purpose. Which in this case is… is…)
*One's identity is not just being gay. One's identity is as a child of God.*
(Agree to agree-ish.)
*This is just one tiny part of him.*
(Agree to disagree.)

## *But Jesus*

Said love everyone,
Treat them kindly, too.
When your heart is filled with love,
Others will love you.

### *Enter to Learn*

*"...nor do we intend to admit to this campus any homosexuals...*
*If any of you have this tendency... may I suggest*
*you leave the University immediately...*
*We do not want others on this campus to be contaminated by your presence."*
- Ernest Wilkinson, President of BYU, 1965

## The Application

MIT
Harvard
Stanford
Columbia
Yale
Princeton
Brown
Berkeley
Oxford
NYU

Will each receive a packet of essays from your son
Their tone humble for a kid who's never made a B in his life
He's got the scores; he checks the boxes
Has led numerous service, leadership, and government clubs
Has lived abroad, traveled to 7 continents and 43 states
Volunteered in a Serbian refugee camp, feeds the homeless every month
Started a program for tutors to help teachers during a pandemic
Earned an Eagle Scout and hiked 100 miles at Philmont
Helped "the one" in clubs like No Place for Hate,
Cool 2 B Kind, Best Buddies
Came out his junior year of high school
after being raised in the religion of his ancestors
Then left said religion to consider
Buddhism, Bahaism, agnosticism. Himself.
It's an essay you wonder how BYU would receive.
BYU: the alma mater of your Cougar blue parents, your
grandparents, your husband, yourself— once upon a time.
The institution that comes with a ward, an FHE group, a safety net.
Yet another mourning, another question—
Rhetorical, as they will never receive this essay from your son.

## Let's Break It Down

So he didn't choose this.
*True.*
He can't change it.
*We believe that.*
Can't "fix it."
*Not really.*
Can't make it go away.
*I'd imagine not.*
You don't encourage a mixed orientation marriage.
*We now acknowledge that might not be best.*
And eternal marriage—the "new and everlasting covenant."
*Yes!*
The dream, desire, mandate, epitomal goal?
*Absolutely!*
What is preached from every pulpit, in every class?
*That is the Plan...*
And faith, hope, charity?
*Cornerstones. Pillars. Foundations.*
Where is his?


Is your marriage and family just one tiny part of you?
Or is it everything that you're told to pursue
From the moment you first meet that pew?
What do you do when you are the fine print,
the exception, the asterisk?
Where do you sit?

## The Best Advice

Comes from a friend
With many reasons of her own:
two siblings, a daughter, her grandson

*Life is a journey and all this time you've been given maps to follow:*
*instructions, handbooks, guides.*
*Especially in our faith journey,*
*we sometimes have to put down our map*
*and pick up our compass.*
*What points us to God is unique and personal.*
*Now you get a compass.*

A compass.
I try out the words:
A compass.
I hand him a white gift bag during his first Pride.
Our first Pride.
He pulls out a gold compass, ordered online, inscribed.
A compass.

## A Mother's Prayer

In a side yard, where the dog runs
You hug your knees on a rusty metal bench
The morning sun reaches through the trees
And warms your tears
It's been some time since he told you
Months of reading and ruminating on the why, when, how
Now your chest heaves with the What
What will you do?
Once the quiet shade of the pandemic lifts
And you must decide whether to return
He's already left
Your husband might follow
You have one on a mission
Two at the tail…
Watching.
You've been given a get out of jail free card
A hall pass
But is it your jail?
What is your jail?
Bloom where you're planted
Pioneer heritage
We can do hard things
How hard will it be to sit on that plush bench without him?
Without them?
Will you go?
Will you wear your rainbow pin?
Will you speak up, speak out?

Raise your hand?

Walk out?

Or whisper, "They just don't know yet," through every testimony.

Is this the place for you?

A voice from above whispers

Words meant just for you

(But not for everybody

If it is indeed their jail.)

But for you, right now, they breathe:

"How will they know if you leave?"

## In Search of Masculine, Manly Men

*"From our pre-mortal life, we were directed into a physical body.*
*There is no mismatching of bodies and spirits.*
*Boys are to become men*—masculine, manly men—
*ultimately to become husbands and father…*
*There is a falsehood that some are born*
*with an attraction to their own kind,*
*with nothing they can do about it.*
*They are just 'that way' and can only yield to those desires.*
*That is a malicious and destructive lie.*
*No one is locked into that kind of life."*
- Elder Boyd K. Packer, 1976

### Not Sure

Anymore
About Jesus
He says
At Christmas
And it breaks your heart.
Did you push too hard
Or not enough?
(The compass is nice, but sometimes you crave a manual.)
He joined family church
But stopped once it streamed online
From pulpits and people
Who before called him "unnatural."
(Or worse.)
You only begged once
For him to join an assembly
You were the speaker
The topic was service
It seemed safe enough
And was, until the keynote from Salt Lake took to the pulpit
And reminded him the church—The Church—was the one way,
the *only* way.
And now
At Christmas
He doesn't want to listen to Silent Night.
But he still closes his eyes
And bows his head
When you pray.

## Masculine, Manly Men

We're walking along Fisherman's Wharf,
It's summer, irony's coldest season.
My husband and younger son lead our traipse through the crowds
The two girls in the middle.
As always, amid the hills and gusts
I fall behind.
Neuropathy has a way of doing that.
Hills and gusts have a way of making it worse.
My drop foot intensifies; my left side drags—
My body entering shutdown mode.
When like an anchor, I feel the warm strength of my oldest son.
He wraps his jacket around my shoulders. His gentle cradle and
outstretched arm support, push, almost pull me up the hill.
He says nothing. He is 14.
The manly men are up ahead, lost in the crowd:
My husband who brags he dated
probably 100 girls before we married.
My charming son who convinced Heidi Klum
to deliver his first kiss (on his cheek).
But it is this son who notices his mother struggling to walk.
*This* one, who was born *that way.*

## The Only Way

Everyone raved about the keynote from Salt Lake
Everyone but your son.
Who afterward wanted to drive off the bridge to mute the
reverberating words

But instead went and met up with a friend—
A girl he once tried to date, tried to like; how he tried
A girl who won't sit for a keynote from Salt Lake
But she smiles with Christ in her eyes every time she enters your space
So full of love
So full for all.
Did he know, that keynote, when he looked your son in the eye—
Knowing he was your son, because you had just told him
Knowing that your son had freshly left "the fold"
Because of all the things he'd been told
By people at a pulpit
Did he have any idea
That by telling him that The. Church. is The. Only. Way.
That what some hear him really say
Is that their prescribed lonely path that often leads to dead ends
Runs parallel to the road that works so well for him and his friends
Until it doesn't
Until it detours
At a bridge. With a gun. Too many pills. A rope.
Where is their hope?

## "The Gay Lifestyle"

Wake up. Flush. Brush your teeth.

Make breakfast, or skip it. Some run late.

Go to work. Work. Laugh with the cubicle next door.

Take a coffee break—or water, if you choose.

On your way home, the musts:

pick up the dry cleaning, the kid(s) perhaps.

Stop by the post office. The gym. The grocery store.

Grab takeout if your favorite show's on.

Watch your favorite show.

Bathe the kid(s). Story time, for them, for you.

Hold hands, feet on each other's laps. Recount the cubicle incident.

Confirm the details for your spring break trip.

Turn out the lights.

The electricity bill was off the charts last month.

Rinse, repeat.

## *Why'd You Join That Gym?*

It's the closest one to my house.
Because my family joined.
I like their classes.
It's so big.
It's small, cozy.
I love the trainers.
I love the equipment.
Easy parking.
You can quit anytime.
Friends.

But the thing about gyms (and churches)…

They don't work unless you do.
They're there to help, not hurt.
They're meant to make you strong, healthy.
What you do the other 22 hours of the day is just as important,
if not more.
You can quit anytime.
You can join a different one.
This new gym might work better for you.
Maybe after an injury, you just need time to recover.
Or maybe you don't need a gym at all.
Maybe you can work out in nature, in your bedroom,
on your knees, by yourself.
When you walk out of a gym that's not working for you,
your well-being leaves with you.
Maybe not everyone needs a gym to get their desired result.

### *A Really Good Samaritan*

You ask the men in charge to take him off the mission prep list.

He will no longer be attending.

(As for you? Undecided.)

You fill them in via text.

The facts, and the reality:

That things have been said.

Some teachings aren't translating.

Kids have been mean.

People need to change.

Perhaps the stake could offer support?

The top brass, the president, who just sent your daughter on a mission,

never responds.

One in his circle begs audience with your son,

to tell him, "We love you, but…" You decline.

But another—

He crosses the dirt road and scoops up your family with his words:

*"I'll walk with you, I'll march with you, anytime you need me."*


And sometimes he is the only reason you still go to that gym.

## A Child's Prayer (2)

*Heavenly Father, I remember now*
*Something that Jesus told disciples long ago:*
*"Suffer the children to come to me."*
*Father, in prayer [he's] coming now to thee...*
In an Airbnb in New Zealand
During a family reunion of 18, hosted by missionary grandparents.
While we counted heaps of sheep and ate Fergburgers
He beat his head against a cold, tile, shower wall
Sobbing, begging, pleading, and finally hearing
*"You matter to me."*
Softly through the steam.
(Too soft?)
But enough to buy one more year
Of silent desperation.

"Our Christianity loves its ease and comfort too well
to take up anything so rough and heavy as a cross."
*I can see that.*
Charles M. Sheldon, a young minister, said that.
*I know.*
Is it true?
*Perhaps.*
What made your cross so heavy? The Garden or the Hill?
*What do you think?*
We're told it's the Garden, the internalized pain spilt in blood.
*Go on.*
The only time in recorded history you complained.
*I did?*
Well, opted out. Or opted to opt out. "Father, if it be thy will,
remove this cup…"
*What if those words weren't said for me, but for you?*
For me?
*For him.*
For Gavin?
*For everyone. Everyone who says it's not fair, why me, please take this away.*
So… we could relate? So you didn't need it to stop?
*I wished it weren't so necessary. It was a lot.*
But you could handle it?
*I am of unique origin.*
Did you not want to do it?
*The important thing is I did.*
For him.
*For everyone.*
Of course. But right now, I'm thinking about him.
How you did it for him.

*I'd do it again only for him.*
*And for you.*


A thank you doesn't seem adequate.
*I don't need thank you notes.*
I imagine the suffering might have been quite a bit less, if just for him.
He's a really good boy.
*Do you know how his heart suffers?*
I know you do.


His life a perpetual round of fear, coming out, hiding, retreating. Is it because of what the kids snickered after they left seminary? Is that his Stonewall? Is this his Lifetime movie? When does it end?


Does he also really want the cup removed? This: his Gethsemane.


*What do you think?*


But it's there so he can be him. Noticing others who struggle to walk. It's there so we can listen and learn. Love. Encircle.


Why do they say those things? They who claim to believe in you? Which side are you on? Whose side are you on? Why did you bleed for him? Why was he made this way if it doesn't fit into the Plan? The Plan since Primary? If it only begets more blood, more tears, more unknowns? Who cast that stone, who thrust that spear? Was it him, was it them? Is it me?


*Your heart suffers.*


Mine is old enough to suffer. Mine will survive. What about his?

### Secrets Make You Sick

Seventeen years of secrets
Naturally make you vomit
"But it's a lifetime of coming out," he said.
Does this make it chronic?
How's he doing? They ask.
And the good ones mean it, I think.
Do you tell them all is well?
Clear your throat, smile, blink
Or tell them he's trying to fast-forward
Life he's (not really) "living" now
While you're on constant rewind
To pinpoint why and how.
He claims life will start the day
He packs up, leaves this town
To finally live his truth
And you won't be around.

## *Bridges*

MIT

Harvard

Stanford

Columbia

Yale

Princeton

Brown

Berkeley

Oxford

NYU

How about adding a safety school?

You ask, hopeful but realistic.

But you think

Why must he pick so many bustling cities

In faraway places

Where bridges are aplenty?

## Never Walked a Mile in Rainbow Shoes

Said a friend from high school
Via Instagram after your Pride month post embracing your son.
She wants to know if you've really read the Bible.
(Again: Which version do the Mormons believe?)
Once upon a time, you did a pageant together
As Tennessee girls do.
She was an artist who wore a chastity ring.
Now she wears a wedding ring and posts pictures
with her kids on vacation in Florida.
She sends you her conviction and invites you to pass it to your son:
A John MacArthur sermon from 1992 in which he calls your son an
evil, vile, repulsive, deviant, sordid, perverted, detestable sinner
who frolics through bath houses
sleeping with 1000 anonymous partners a year.
He lines him up with murderers, rapists, and pedophiles
and scorns his "gay agenda."
Her religion makes yours look like a rainbow parade.
You mute her, all of her.
Because to unfollow would be rude (bless her heart).
Your son will not be applying to any safety schools in Tennessee.
No offense, Tennessee.

## "The Gay Agenda"

To drive.

To sit.

To park.

To travel.

To work.

To go to the doctor.

To love.

To get married.

To have a family.

To earn an income.

To bike.

To fly.

To mourn.

To comfort.

To not be alone.

To sign.

To pay bills.

To cohabit.

To attend.

To be let in.

To bury.

To inherit.

To breathe.

To laugh.

To smile.

Without fear.

## A Mother's Prayer (2)

Heavenly Father, Mother, sweet Jesus, angels, ancestors,
Is anyone there
Who can answer this child's prayer?
Because he's stopped saying them.
There were years of them
Are they stored?
Or discarded?
What about
His mother's prayers?

# But Has He Read This?

*"Marriage should not be viewed as a way to solve homosexual problems. The lives of others should not be damaged by entering a marriage where such concerns exist. Encouraging members to cultivate heterosexual feelings as a way to resolve homosexual problems generally leads them to frustration and discouragement."*
- President Gordon B. Hinckley, 1992

## Wait! So Does That Mean...
*(No.) The doctrine doesn't change.\**

## What About When...
*"Black skin is a sign of divine disfavor or curse..."*
*"Black skin reflects unrighteous actions in pre-mortal life..."*
*"Mixed-race marriages are a sin..."*
- Brigham Young, Bruce R. McConkie, Mark E. Peterson

## Became This...
*"Church leaders now unequivocally condemn all racism, past and present, in any form."*
- The LDS Church Website, present day

## One Explanation
*"I don't know that it's possible to distinguish between policy and doctrine in a church that believes in continuing revelation and sustains its leader as a prophet... I'm not sure I could justify the difference in doctrine and policy in the fact that before 1978 a person could not hold the priesthood and after 1978 they could hold the priesthood..."*
- President Dallin H. Oaks, 1988

Dear Autumn Ridge neighbor and ward member,

Hopefully, you will read the following in the spirit that it is offered. It is not intended to be contentious or to cause bad feelings. Recently flags of the LGBT community were flown in our neighborhood which is concerning to many of us. Therefore, please ask yourself the following questions.

Is choosing to fly the colors of the LGBT community consistent with the covenants you made with God as a member of the Church of Jesus Christ of Latter Day Saints? Have you considered the message that you are sending to your non-member neighbors? Will a casual observer know or appreciate that you are trying to draw attention to gay teen suicide? Can you love and support your neighbor and others without flying a flag that actively promotes a lifestyle that is out of alignment with God's plan for the family? Are you aware of what the "Gay Pride" flag stands for? Are their values, your values? If you are unsure about any of these questions, please conduct a prayerful search to obtain your answers.

Also ask yourself, do I demonstrate the values of the church and do I honor the covenants that I made to follow the teachings of the church and Christ? Take notice of the ward members who did *not* agree to have flags placed in their yards, including our Bishop and his Counselors who are setting the example that we all should follow.

If you decide that temple attendance is an important part of your worship, and if you decide to receive or renew a temple recommend, try to truthfully answer the following question.

**7. Do you support or promote any teachings, practices, or doctrine contrary to those of The Church of Jesus Christ of Latter-day Saints?** Can you truthfully say that you do not support or promote a contrary doctrine when you fly the colors of an organization that is clearly inconsistent with these practices?

These are the observations of concerned neighbors and fellow members who desire to share our point of view. You are blessed with moral agency, and you are obviously free to act in a manner consistent with your agency. Just consider if highlighting your agency in such a public way is how you want to be known or remembered.

Sincerely,

Your Autumn Ridge neighbors and ward members

An actual letter sent to residents of the
Autumn Ridge neighborhood of Sandy, UT in Oct 2020.

## The Brave, Anonymous Letter of Autumn Ridge

Was not very brave at all
In its anonymity
Signed with concern
And Judgment
The writer posturing as more than one
(Where do the cowards meet? After Sunday School? Or during?)
They could have ripped out the flags themselves
After taking their kids toilet papering one night
But that would have sacrificed their ability to preach propriety
And remove your agency.
Remember it is you who is choosing Satan's plan
With all your rainbow waving.
With all your "tolerance."
They type that you support gay suicide
(Was it a typo?
Because isn't it them?)
They remind you of your covenants
Broken
As you wave tall and proud
As you beckon the One
To sneak out their window
And knock on your door to sleep on your couch
Instead of tying a noose in their garage.
It makes the news, this brave letter
And they never get their 15 seconds
Of Righteousness.
Because, Anonymous

He buckles over in the barstool at the counter
Mentally emaciated after four days of essay prompts
He wants it so bad
To earn that sweatshirt he's worn for the past three years: "MIT"
He leaves it around town
Friends always know whose doorstep to leave it on
I hand him some pills. (No, not that kind.)
SAMe, B12; a swipe of frankincense on the back of his neck
I imbue their promise and placebo
And remind him it's almost over.
I think back to our college tour
To his dream, the top engineering school in the world
My son who's filled our garage with Lego masterpieces
(one of his essays)
Now wants to fill his mind with MIT.
A student from an upstate farm town of 600 gave us the tour.
In her hometown, kids drove tractors to a schoolhouse
And they had no AP/IB program or honors.
(Would love to read her essays.)
She praised the pass/fail freshman year incentive
No pressure of As for these students
who had never earned anything but
It pushed them into new pursuits:
Ballet, art history, German
She picked up a humanities minor from the experiment
She lauds the clubs, the pranks, or "hacks,"
Admits studying outweighs the social
And hurries through the bit about the suicide rate,
among the highest in the nation
Brought on by the pressure of all the others

who've never earned less than an A
And that is all you will remember
As your son bangs his head against the counter
And cries he must succeed in this one realm.
He must show those who no longer talk to him
he's worthy of something.
He must leave them all behind.
He must go to MIT.

# Excerpts from *A Conversation with a General Authority…*

It's kind of like coffee. 99% of the world's favorite drink:
a staple, a ritual.

*How's that?*

I didn't grow up drinking it; never even wanted to.

*Obedience.*

Perhaps. Also, I never liked the taste. But that's the thing: 99% of the
world did grow up drinking it, loving it, can't even fathom giving it up.

*Sure.*

And thus 99% of the world won't listen to why they might or should.

*It's about obedience.*

For them? Or for us?

*Precept by precept.*

But faith precedes obedience.

*True.*

When the missionaries knock, they won't even open the door
because of the coffee.

When they hear the words "LDS, Mormon," they think coffee.

*Sacrifice.*

Before they've ever heard of the law of sacrifice.

*It's a code of health.*

But does it keep you from salvation?

*Of course not!*

But it keeps them from opening the door. From Christ's church,
intended for all. A beverage.

Not too different from your Diet Coke or Red Bull.

*Perhaps…*

So back to The Plan of Happiness. Eternal marriage. Eternal families.

*Much more important.*

And you love yours?

*They're my everything.*

As they should be.

And marriage: ordained to be between one man, one woman.

*Doctrine. Unchanging. God's Plan.*

For all but 3-13% of God's children, pending the survey.

*For all. Your son's identity is not gay, his identity is a child of God.*

*Some may feel…*

It's not for them? Because currently, it's not. This 3-13% —

*It's a higher law.*

What about the 3-13% brought up in this quest for obedience?
Implanted since Sunbeams with a sunny plan that crumbles when
they realize their biology doesn't fit the plan? When they realize the
end goal is unachievable in this life, and there's no surety about what
comes next? It makes sense the truest of believers
might see suicide as the safest way out.

*There are things we do not yet fully understand.*

Are we asking?

*I do not tell God what to do.*

But are we asking?

*The doctrine doesn't change.*

Hasn't it, though? What about polygamy? The priesthood ban?

How does their marriage attack yours or mine?

And if it doesn't

Then why not err on the side of caution, in their favor?

Why not let people keep their coffee?

If God's plan is for everyone?

## One Youth Leader

Said: *"Glad we got rid of the liberal fag"*

In reference to the beloved seminary teacher who's moving.
The same beloved teacher who kept your son going to seminary
by saying we need to make more room for people like him
before he ever even knew the truth about your son.
That seminary teacher was your son's first call
the day after he came out to you
that night at 3 a.m.
And at 3 a.m that night
when your son told you he would not be
going to church anymore it was because this
beloved seminary teacher was moving (for a job transfer)
and your son no longer felt safe at church without him there.
So just like that, the youth leader rid himself
of two "liberal fags" in one shot.
Collateral damage.

## Collateral Damage

On Sunday mornings, I tiptoe.
The first year ever I'm grateful for 8:30 a.m. church.
Luckily, a teen—he still sleeps.
Most weeks it's still too hard
To leave one behind to take the rest back
Now that the doors have reopened.
He came out during quarantine
Allowing us all rest.
(God's COVID mercy.)
Sundays are still for families.
He's still a part of us.
(Mercy.)
I can stay home and still find a meeting on zoom.
I can find church on my phone.
I can sing along with Lauren Daigle.
We've moved to a new ward
With many who refused to wear masks
But it is you who needs to do better at following the prophet.
Some of their kids were the ones, those ones
Who tried to get the beloved seminary teacher fired.
I prescreen the program each week
Who's speaking?
Who's teaching?
Are we safe?
But it's not about me
Because I am a mother.
I have two younger teens
Who still want it, need it
Most weeks they wake up ready to go.
And we slip into the back row.

My husband, our guard dog, has found
So many new reasons to call in sick on Sundays.
So often it is just the youngers and I
And when I have to walk out and finish church
Bleary-eyed in a parking lot, my mask now a tissue
My Sunday School a podcast
They understand why.
It's not because of the kid Gavin's age
Who got up and gave his mission farewell
I'm happy for him, really.
I have a missionary, too.
It's because we cannot find a seat in the overflow.
Even our back row is taken
Bustling with droves of kids Gavin's age
Who used to come to our house
But don't anymore.
And today they have shown up to support another friend
Living their mutual LDS dream.
While my son sleeps at home
And walks alone.

# *Waitlisted*

"I didn't get in," he says, shrugs.
And walks away from that crimson MIT letterhead.
But wait, you're deferred—waitlisted! I see:
Hope!
Then I see the harm in the hope
As he turns back and looks at me with hard, dark eyes
A kid who's tired of waiting
A kid who feels safer now
in hopelessness.

## It's Like Going to That Restaurant...

The one that's the talk of the town
(A new friend tells me—with a rainbow child of her own)
And you get there and the reviews have promised everything
Is amazing, they've got a Michelin chef, the hype is real
And you're there with your family, ogling the entrees
Your server laughs you can't go wrong
And everyone picks and chooses
Around the table
In a circle
Asparagus fries,
Lettuce wraps, risotto, lamb,
Filet, lobster. And then the server points at
Your child—the one there on the end. He stops him
Before he can order and says Wait. Everyone can eat here but you.
But you're welcome to stay and sit and watch. I can bring you a water
(While they pass around warm, buttery sourdough
and share chocolate cake.)
But he's hungry, too.
What would you do?
Do you stay and eat?
Or do you leave?

# The Marines Called

He's not interested.
*Might I ask why not?*
We love the Marines.
*Thank you, ma'am.*
My grandpa was a Marine.
*Oorah.*
Semper fi.
*Semper fi. So...*
So.
*Why wouldn't your son want to hear more?*
You really want to know?
*Of course.*
Well... he's gay. I don't think he'd be comfortable there. You get me?
*I see, ma'am.*
Don't ask, don't tell. He tells now.
*I hear you.*


Gavin, the Marines called and I told them you weren't interested
because... you're gay.
Why didn't you just tell them I was a pacifist?
That wasn't the first thing that came to mind. I'm new at this. Sorry.


Would you rather send a pacifist son to war
or a gay son to military barracks?
More things I think at 3 a.m.

# I Loved to See the Temple

I really did.
Even when people pontificated on the strange.
I saw what they meant
But still welcomed the 90 minutes of quiet communion
No pings or notifications allowed
Only the divine.
I loved the blueprints, the plans –
That we were all part of a plan.
Even if I don't know how that plan ends for us anymore.
But that's the thing, isn't it, there isn't an end
And we are so early in our story, so much to come
*Progression.*

A friend hands me a golden ticket during lockdown—
An invitation to witness her endowment
And I ask myself in what tense do I want to see the temple
Packed away to remember all the good I once felt?
Preserved as a place for others to enjoy in the future, but not for me?
Or enter in my current state, unsure what parts I believe anymore
And if it's even necessary, if not meant for all.
*Quiet communion…*

You promise. I acquiesce. And arrive.
And sit in a quiet, dimly lit room with a handful of imperfect people
Who love each other imperfectly.
I brace myself for what might come and shatter whatever's left
Of all I've ever believed.
I observe Eve, with her impossible choice,
The contradictory commands.
 I observe things have changed, because good things are supposed to

An action, a picture, a phrase now improved.
And I plead for something new
That might solve everything.
But instead, I receive words I've heard before,
Only this time they beat like a drum. A mantra.

*All are alike unto God.*
*It is not good for man to be alone.*
*Men are that they might have joy.*

And I gasp in my quiet communion
And open my eyes to the bright light
As I take it all in
The love
The hope
The mercy
That always was
And remains to be
For him, for all, for me.

## Invisible

He toggles between
What he knew, what he now knows
Both spaces hollow
Only a few of the kids from the overflow
Still call his name
Still know his number
When they gather, no one's sure what to say.
He wades into dating
And it makes you so happy
To see him fix his hair like he cares.
You secretly hope he meets the guy (a high schooler, you checked)
Two towns north
Because you're not sure they'd be safe here in your town.
He must sense this already, because he does.
And that week in your life
As you gather with friends from church who prattle on
About their kids, their kids' plans, their kids' dates,
You know better than to mention your son's first (real) one
Even though it made you both smile.

## *The Resource*

I get calls now, about once a week
From a compassionate leader, a panicked mom, a trembling youth:
How can we love better? What do I do? Will my parents kick me out?
I listen. I learn. I love.
I ask questions.
I don't remind them about keeping the commandments.
They know about the commandments.
Plus. There is actually no commandment that…
I send over my list:
The books, the podcasts, the research, the statistics.
Therapists' phone numbers, support groups,
The suicide prevention line.
They will need it all.
I do not send the church's website
They have already been to the church's website.
There is still so little on this page of the church's website.

We are the resources.

And to the 25-year-old who called last month, worried his parents
will delete him from the family, because they preemptively told him
as much when they found his phone a decade ago. He's ready to take
that risk. He cannot do this anymore. He cannot hide forever, alone.

His mother also called, wants to do lunch again next week. The
mother who has asked polite questions about my son over the past
year. I sense her curiosity. I sense she is being prepared. Yet now I
also know what she once said to her son behind closed doors.

## *Active*

Or activist? What are you now?
And where does your husband lean?
He circles your son, a single-minded fortress
While you try to change the world
For all the upcoming Gavins.
You write weekly family profiles online:
How to Lift, How to Love
@liftandloveorg
Meeting hundreds of families just like yours.
Their pearls resonate:

*"You have to affirm yourself and believe in your own goodness."*

*"It's more important to avoid breaking a person than to avoid breaking a rule."*

*"I plead that you be more understanding to people who experience and struggle
with things that you may not experience and understand for yourself."*

*"There are too many people—and too great of people—to have this in their
lives for no reason."*

*"I want to stick around and be here—the woman with the rainbow pin. The one
who raises her hand and reminds people that things have changed;
leaders don't say those things anymore."*

*"It just makes you mad when you're in a church that works so well for you, but
there's no place for your child. When we don't make space for our LGBTQ
kids, we're also not making space for the people who love them."*

*"To ask another human being to live their whole life without a companion when you have one? That's just cruel."*

*"I don't believe in a Heavenly Father who would make you the way you are then punish you for being that way."*

*"We were given this family on earth for a reason and if we turn our backs on our children because they are doing something we don't like, then we just failed our test here on earth."*

*"I separate the church from the gospel. My gay children are light seekers and bearers and do it a lot better than a lot of Christians. This is a blessing, not a trial. The trial is seeing them in pain."*

*"We as a church have failed our LGBTQ members. We have a lot of work to do. We need to listen to and understand them, and we need to let them know they belong."*

*"We don't belong here. We don't belong anywhere. And so we mourn. Alone. There is no plan in place for families like ours. Let's push for further light and knowledge regarding our LGBTQ family members."*

*"We are the opposite of lazy learners or lax disciples. True eternal success won't be because of a temple recommend; it will be because we loved unconditionally."*

## This Is the Place

Acceptance letters arrive.
The safety schools come through. But none excite him.
Your son's name (and your hope) sits on waitlists at
MIT, Harvard, Brown.
Possibilities.
But not sure things.
He wants the sure thing.
He's worked so hard for a promising sure thing.
It comes on a Tuesday afternoon
He runs out of his room in his socks and
slides across the wooden floor:
"Berkeley! I got into Berkeley!"
And you summon your compass and wrap your head around that.
Berkeley.
(A top-tier school.)
Berkeley.
(436 miles north.)
Berkeley.
(A one-hour flight.)
And it feels right.
To you, your husband, your son.
You all nod. Smile. Laugh.
Berkeley.
His path.
You excitedly text a friend whose graduate
is one of the 48 kids from the overflow
Headed to Provo
And she replies, "So bummed he won't be in Utah!"

### Prom

He's so bummed it's in Utah.
But senior prom is no sure thing in COVID, California.
Like last year's junior one. And every kid deserves a prom.
So he agrees to go with your college roommate's lovely daughter.
(Even though she's a girl. Even though she's a girl who lives in Utah.)
A whole weekend at a Utah prom with a group date
Of Utah kids he doesn't know.
His date says she doesn't know them that well either.
One of the boys in the group texts him:
"Faggot. Faggot! When are you flying in? Speak, faggot."
He comes home from school with that in his pocket on a Friday
Right before he's about to board the plane to Utah.
And he doesn't tell you about the texts
Just that he really doesn't want to go.
But you see the texts.
Your heart drops
And you burn down their houses in your mind
(Do they also live in Autumn Ridge?)
And you watch him gracefully text his date, "Do they know I'm gay?"
And she replies, "I'm so sry, thought u were out!
But it's nbd, they're lgbtq, too!"
And you see his shoulders lift, and the life in his eyes return
As he processes that internalized homophobia
Manifests itself in weird ways in Utah.
And you realize that his date, this gem, picked a group not for her,
But for him
So that he might be comfortable.
And he goes, and he is.
Time-of-his-life comfortable.
In Heber City, Utah.

## His Path

You decide to visit, just to make sure
(With your compass.)
The night before, you dream of graffiti-covered bridges.
In the morning, the three of you embark, 436 miles to the north
You drive up and down the hills of Berkeley, a tree-lined city
Near the cold bay where your son once helped you walk a steep hill
The sun breaks through the fog
Hikers hike, bikers bike
You meet a bell-bottomed cousin for lunch
Who prefers to walk everywhere
And cares about humanity and Mother Earth the way Gavin does.
You order kale and quinoa at a sidewalk café.
You pass record shops, thrift stores,
The cozy bungalows of professors
And former scholars who have made this their forever home.
Nearly every yard hosts a rainbow flag and informs you that, here,
Black lives matter.
In the rearview mirror, your son settles into his seat
And exhales the bated breath
Of a lifetime of excruciating 3 a.m.s.
On campus, you encounter graduates in gowns
Taking final pictures with friends.
And you sense many of them know 3 a.m., too
Now, they gush how they LOOOVED their time at Cal.
You slip your compass into your pocket. As does he.
It is a perfect day.
It is not until you are back on the plane that you realize
The only bridges you saw
Were far away in the distance
Perhaps for good.

## *Muskets*

His first day at Berkeley is an adventure.
He's awoken by a fire alarm; someone's burnt toast.
All are evacuated and will stand outside for two hours in the cold.
Half will remain in pajamas for their first day of class.
The homeless encampment across the street at People's Park
has also chosen this day to stage a protest against the land developer
seeking to dismantle their tent city.
They block all entrances to campus,
including professors from parking.
Meanwhile, on campus, the vegans protest
the distribution of animal products
by strewing decapitated stuffed animals around the lawn
and pouring fake blood in the fountains.
Your son calls you to report on his first day.
Slightly humored by it all.

One week later, you drive your returned missionary daughter to BYU
Where the men's hair is as well-manicured as the lawns,
and no beards allowed.
An apostle known for speaking hope and love has taken his place
at a podium and accuses a former valedictorian of commandeering
that same podium. But the latter is deemed a nuisance because he
dared to share his orientation in a pre-approved speech
where so many scholars and apostles before have shared charming
anecdotes about their kids and gratitude for their spouses.
Hardly "divisive," because they fit the standard. They are the norm.
The apostle commandeers faithful warriors
to take up figurative musket fire
against those (like you) who dare to advocate for those (like your son),
whose very presence makes the majority feel under attack.

55

Each school's first week will make headline news.
Each university shakes their head at the other.
You have delivered these two children into this world,
to these schools:
One where "the ungodly" protest for humanity and animals
One where "the godly" protest against humans like your son
You exhale, knowing at which school your son is safe.
He made the right choice.

You question it all, everything.

# Whiplash

*"I think we've all had—all aspects, all elements of society—including ourselves have gained added understanding... especially in recent years as we've seen... more communication—back and forth, more sharing, more openness on all sides... And there are the science issues... the social science and the physical science and all the other pieces to the puzzle that are coming into focus... There are still a lot of questions... So we're seeking added understanding... We are still learning, we think, and I hope everyone feels that way."*

- Elder D. Todd Christofferson, 2015

*"I can imagine that in most circumstances the parents would say, 'Please don't do that. Don't put us into that position.' Surely if there are children in the home who would be influenced by this example, the answer would likely be that. There would also be other factors that would make that the likely answer. I can also imagine some circumstances in which it might be possible to say, 'Yes, come, but don't expect to stay overnight. Don't expect to be a lengthy house guest. Don't expect us to take you out and introduce you to our friends, or to deal with you in a public situation that would imply our approval of your 'partnership.'"*

- Elder Dallin H. Oaks, 2006

*"We need to listen to and understand what our LGBT brothers and sisters are feeling and experiencing. Certainly, we must do better than we have done in the past so that all members feel they have a spiritual home where their brothers and sisters love them and where they have a place to worship and serve the Lord."*

- Elder Russell M. Ballard, 2017

*"Remember, it was the questions young Joseph asked that opened the door for the restoration of all things. We can block the growth and knowledge our Heavenly Father intends for us. How often has the Holy Spirit tried to tell us something we needed to know but couldn't get past the massive iron gate of what we thought we already knew?"*

- Elder Dieter F. Uchtdorf, 2017

Soon after the lifting of the priesthood and temple ban for Black saints: *"Forget everything that I have said, or what President Brigham Young or whomsoever has said in days past that is contrary to the present revelation. We spoke with a limited understanding and without the light and knowledge that now has come into the world."*

- Elder Bruce R. McConkie, 1978

Regarding the priesthood and temple ban at the "Be One" celebration: *"I observed the pain and frustration experienced by those who suffered these restrictions and those who criticized them and sought for reasons. I studied the reasons then being given and could not feel confirmation of the truth of any of them."*

- Elder Dallin H. Oaks, 2018

*"It is important to remember that I am a General Authority, but that does not make me an authority in general! My calling and life experiences allow me to respond to certain types of questions. There are other types of questions that require an expert in a specific subject matter. This is exactly what I do when I need an answer to such questions: I seek help from others, including those with degrees and expertise in such fields."*

- Elder M. Russell Ballard, 2017

*"Prophets are yet mortal men with imperfections common to mankind in general. They have their opinions and prejudices and are left to work out their problems without inspiration in many instances."*

- Elder Bruce R. McConkie, 2007

*"I am more afraid that this people have so much confidence in their leaders that they will not inquire for themselves of God whether they are led by him. I am fearful they settle down in a state of blind self-security, trusting their eternal destiny in the hands of their leaders with a reckless confidence that in itself would thwart the purposes of God in their salvation, and weaken that influence they could give to their leaders, did they know for themselves, by the revelations of Jesus, that they are led in the right way. Let every man and woman know, by the whispering of the Spirit of God to themselves, whether their leaders are walking in the path the Lord dictates, or not."*

- President Brigham Young, 1862

*"We sometimes don't believe truth or reject it—because it would require us to change or admit that we were wrong. Often, truth is rejected because it doesn't appear to be consistent with previous experiences... Yes, we do have the fulness of the everlasting gospel, but that does not mean that we know everything. In fact, one principle of the restored gospel is our belief that God 'will yet reveal many great and important things.'"*

- Elder Dieter F. Uchtdorf, 2013

*"God makes them the way they come, and God don't make no mistakes."*

- My father-in-law, Len McAlpin, 2020

## But Jesus Said

*He that is without sin among you, let him cast the first stone.*

*Thou shalt love the Lord thy God will all thy heart, and with all thy soul, and with all thy mind, and with all thy strength: this is the first commandment. And the second is like, namely this, Thou shalt love thy neighbor as thyself. There is none other commandment greater than these.*

*A new command I give unto you, That ye love one another; as I have loved you, that ye also love one another.*

*Let not your heart be troubled, neither let it be afraid.*

*Blessed are ye, when men shall revile you and persecute you, and shall say all manner of evil against you falsely, for my sake.*

*Whoever will exalt himself will be humbled, and whoever will humble himself will be exalted.*

*And he inviteth them all to come unto him and partake of his goodness; and he denieth none that come unto him, black and white, bond and free, male and female; and he remembereth the heathen; and all are alike unto God, both Jew and Gentile.*

*In my Father's house are many mansions: if it were not so, I would have told you. I go to prepare a place for you.*

*Ask and it shall be given you; seek, and you shall find; knock and it shall be opened unto you.*

### A Mother's Final Prayer

*Heavenly Father, are you really there?*
*And do you hear and answer every [mother's] prayer?*

I (silently) scream, my knuckles now bloody.

And I roll over, and clasp my compass
And rejoice that he is still with us
Mine to love.
So easy to love.
They embody love.
*And their mothers knew it.*

They're here to teach us how to love
As Christ did:
The outcast
The leper
The Pharisee
The One
Father, forgive us, for we know not what we've done.

May they forgive us.

# Epilogue

Gavin would want you to know he is doing well.

Thriving, even.

He has found his place.

He has found his people.

Outside the LDS fold.

He still cannot step foot in a church building without trembling.

There is no healthy place for him there at this time.

Yet it is through him that we have come to know Jesus.

## Acknowledgements

Thank you to the rainbow mamas who opened your arms on day one, ready to listen, hold, guide, and love: Natalie, Jill, Allison, Carol, Val, Jackie, Garnett, Michelle, and so many others who've blazed this path. Carol, thank you for introducing me to the beauty of a compass. Natalie, thank you for challenging us to reconsider where we dine. And Val, you made it all so simple: Just Love.

To my publisher, Adrienne Quintana, who embraced my vision for this book and brought it to life in the most perfect, beautiful way. Thank you for your generosity of spirit in making this possible. And thank you to Marnae for your excellent eagle eye.

To J. Kirk Richards, whose brush strokes on this book cover magnify the heartache, longing, wisdom, and divine purpose of so many mothers who cleave to their inner compasses. How did you know? This is more than I could have dreamed. Thank you for this stunning gift.

To Janice Kapp Perry who gave us so many loving, comfortable words and melodies like "A Child's Prayer" that we can return to in our darkest hours. And to her son, John Perry, thank you for being you, for being here, and for understanding it all.

To Stephenie Larsen, founder of Encircle, thank you for building sacred spaces that literally save lives. You have taken up the cross in desperately needed ways. It is an honor to learn from you.

To Allison Dayton, who helms Lift + Love, thank you for being the first call for so many and for giving of your heart and time. Thank you for granting me space to tell the stories. And to all the lovely humans who share their lives and families with us in this forum—I've learned so much from you.

To the wordsmiths who've shown up to teach this masterclass—especially to Richard Ostler, Pastor Stan Mitchell, Patrick Mason, Becky Edwards, Mike Secrist, Evan Smith, Cynthia Winward, Carol Lynn Pearson, Tom Christofferson, Derek Knox, James Jones, Amy Allebest, Gregory Prince, Charlie Bird, Ben Schilaty, and Jill Hazard Rowe. You are my Sunday School. I'll walk with you—always, anywhere.

To the angels in our town, who appeared on dark days when you didn't know just how much we needed you: Brent Thurgood, Scott Smith, Darren Harline, Dave Budge, Sarah Davis, Mary Alice Hatch, Troy Bourne, and Jon McGee. In some ways, it means more because you often did it in Sunday dress.

To my dear friends who read and witnessed the reality of these pages every day, especially Jen, Nicole, Heather, Amy, and Cara—thank you for having our backs. And to all my soul sisters in our Just Love tribe—you know who you are. I treasure our circle.

To all the stone catchers who sit in classrooms and pews and stand up when needed—oh how we need you.

To all those who've pulled away from my family, I thank you as well. It takes opposition to grow. Growth is good. I invite you to lean in; I am now strong enough to do the same. It's hard to hate up close.

To every single member of our extended family who embraced Gavin from the moment he shared his news over zoom—your haven of love and support is a rare gift, for which I'm eternally grateful. This is family.

To Alex, our firstborn and most vocal in-house ally long before we knew how much we needed her to be. To Blake, who "knew it all along" and decides every day he's not too cool to just love. To Gracie, who's threatened to annihilate anyone who messes with her older brother. And to Manny, who showed up on the scene and was Gavin's friend from day one. You are the best kids. Thank you for your protective force field and for your patience and love as we figure it all out together.

And to our bonus children, who sometimes need a safe space to land—there's always room on our couch.

To Michael. Who knew that this would be the thing... I've loved watching you show up as your authentic self, in all the ways. I love to watch you defend us all with everything in you. There's no one I'd rather have by my side.

To my Gavin. The "smart one." The "most kind." I have a feeling you signed us up for this journey, to teach us all how to love a little better. I'm sorry for all you've suffered and for any ways I've failed you. I'm grateful for all we've learned. You have filled my life with joy. There is so much joy to come.

And most of all, to Jesus. Thank you for the ongoing conversation.

## *About the Author*

A graduate of BYU's English Teaching program and USC's Master of Professional Writing program, Autumn has worked as a writer and filmmaker for the past two decades. Her award-winning feature films, *Waffle Street* and *Miss Arizona,* can be found on iTunes and Amazon, and her stage play, *In Front of the Children*, was awarded first place in USC's Writing for Stage and Screen Competition in 2015.

Photo by Johnny Beutler

Autumn is the author of graduation gift book, *Real World 101: A Survival Guide to Life After High School,* and she penned the humor column, Cracking Up, for *The Orange County Register* for nearly a decade. Autumn currently writes the weekly family profile stories for Lift & Love, a site that serves as an intersection for LDS and LGBTQ+ families. She is also actively engaged with Encircle, a nonprofit that provides safe spaces for LGBTQ+ kids. Autumn grew up in Memphis, TN, and now resides in southern California with her husband and five kids.

Made in the USA
Las Vegas, NV
25 September 2023

78098084R10044